# Animal Family Albums

# Rabbits

Charlotte Guillain

Raintree

Raintree is an imprint of Capstone Global Library
Limited, a company incorporated in England and Wales
having its registered office at 7 Pilgrim Street, London,
EC4V 6LB – Registered company number: 6695582

www.raintreepublishers.co.uk
myorders@raintreepublishers.co.uk

Text © Capstone Global Library Limited 2013
First published in hardback in 2013
First published in paperback in 2014
The moral rights of the proprietor have been asserted.

Edited by Nancy Dickmann and Laura Knowles
Designed by Philippa Jenkins
Original illustrations © Clare Elsom
Illustrations by Clare Elsom
Picture research by Liz Alexander
Originated by Capstone Global Library Ltd
Printed and bound in China by CTPS

ISBN 978 1 406 24959 0 (hardback)
16 15 14 13 12
10 9 8 7 6 5 4 3 2 1

ISBN 978 1 406 24964 4 (paperback)
17 16 15 14 13
10 9 8 7 6 5 4 3 2 1

**British Library Cataloguing in Publication Data**
Guillain, Charlotte.
Rabbits. -- (Animal family albums)
599.3'2-dc23
A full catalogue record for this book is available from
the British Library.

**Acknowledgements**
We would like to thank the following for permission
to reproduce photographs: Alamy pp. 17 (© Ed
Simons), 24 (© Kevin Schafer); Getty Images pp. 8
(GK Hart/Vikki Hart/Photodisc), 21 (David & Micha
Sheldon/F1online); Nature Picture Library pp. 15
(© Jane Burton), 16 (© Eric Baccega), 18 (© Mark
Taylor), 25 (© David Welling); NHPA pp. 4 (William
Paton), 27 (A.N.T. Photo Library); Shutterstock
pp. 5 (© BestPhotoPlus), 6 (© Russell Shively),
7 (© 2009fotofriends), 9 (© Alistair Scott), 10
(© Eric Isselée), 11 (© yykkaa), 12 (© Linn Currie),
19 (© Vishnevskiy Vasily), 22 (© Marina Jay), 23
(© Anikakodydkova), 26 (© wim claes); SuperStock
pp. 13 (© age footstock), 14 (© Juniors), 20 (© age
footstock).

Design elements reproduced with permission
of Shutterstock/© urfin (pencil); Shutterstock/
© Julia Ivantsova (pencil); Shutterstock/© Studio
DMM Photography, Designs & Art (photo corners);
Shutterstock/©Varts (lettuce leaf); Shutterstock/
© sayhmog (orange leather background);
Shutterstock/© Losswen (orange pattern
background).

Cover photographs of rabbits reproduced with
permission of Shutterstock/© Eric Isselée (English
Angora rabbit); Shutterstock/© Vishnevskiy Vasily
(Miniature Lop rabbit); iStockphoto/© Alyn Hunter
(Black Standard Rex rabbit).
Every effort has been made to contact copyright
holders of material reproduced in this book. Any
omissions will be rectified in subsequent printings if
notice is given to the publisher.

# Contents

Some words are printed in bold, **like this**. You can find out what they mean by looking in the glossary.

# Meet the family!

Welcome to the rabbit family album! My name is Nibbles. Let me introduce you to some of my many relatives.

In the wild, hundreds of rabbits can live together in a **warren**.

Rabbits have been around for millions of years. They started out as wild animals before humans started keeping them. At first, people kept rabbits for their meat and fur. But by the 1900s, humans realized what great pets rabbits can be. There are still many rabbits living in the wild all over the world, in big groups called nests or colonies.

# Relative differences

There are many different **breeds** of pet rabbit. A breed is a group of rabbits that look very alike and behave in a certain way. Some have small ears that stick up straight, while others have huge floppy ears! Some rabbits are big and fluffy, while others are little with short fur. But all rabbits have certain things in common. They all have twitching noses and sharp front teeth. And all pet rabbits need a big **run** to exercise in.

## FAMILY SECRET

Hares and jackrabbits aren't rabbits, but they are relatives. Hares have longer ears and back legs than rabbits. A jackrabbit is actually a type of hare!

Rabbits make intelligent and friendly pets.

# A day in our life

Rabbits are most active in the morning and evening. That's when we like to eat!

Wild rabbits mainly eat grass and small plants but they also need to eat their own poo to get more **nutrients**.

Wild rabbits dig a network of burrows (tunnels) under ground, where they sleep for much of the day. Pet rabbits need a large hutch with newspaper and wood shavings on the floor, and an outdoor **run**. They make a nest of **hay**, where they sleep. Just as wild rabbits live in large groups, pet rabbits like to have company, so it's best to keep two or more.

# Rabbit care

Rabbits need to have a good supply of fresh water to drink, as well as clean **bedding**. Rabbits clean themselves using their teeth and tongue but you can also brush a pet rabbit's fur. Unlike humans, rabbits' front teeth never stop growing, so they need to chew and gnaw a lot to keep their teeth the right length.

Pet rabbits eat special dried food, hay, and leafy green vegetables.

# Popular pets

There are so many different **breeds** of pet rabbit. These rabbits are called "Fancy" and you might see them at pet shows.

The white band of fur at the top of a Dutch rabbit's body is called the saddle.

## Dutch rabbits

Dutch rabbits are popular pets. They are medium-sized with short hair and rounded bodies. Dutch rabbits are gentle and don't mind being **handled**. They can be different colours but always have white fur around the top of their body, their toes, and a **blaze** of white on their face.

# New Zealand White rabbits

The New Zealand White is a large rabbit that was originally bred for meat and fur. Today it is a popular pet. The New Zealand White can weigh around 5 kilograms (11 pounds). It has thick and soft pure white fur. This rabbit has a short neck with straight, furry ears with rounded tips, and pink eyes. It is friendly and loves being around people, although it can get too big for children to pick up!

## FAMILY SECRET

New Zealand rabbits don't actually come from New Zealand! In fact, the first of these rabbits were bred in North America.

More New Zealand White rabbits are kept around the world than any other breed.

# Fluffy bunnies

Here are some of my more long-haired relatives! Someone pass me a comb...

Angora rabbits don't make good pets because their coats need so much attention. People keep them for show and exhibitions.

## Angora rabbits

Bunnies don't come much fluffier than this! Angora rabbits are named after the Angora goat because of their long hair. The rabbits were bred for their hair, which was made into warm clothes in southeast France. Today there are several Angora rabbit **breeds**. French Angora rabbits are large, with very long, thick hair, while English Angora rabbits are smaller and have softer, silkier coats.

# Lionhead rabbits

Lionhead rabbits sound scarier than they look! They get their name because they have a mane like an African lion. But this little rabbit isn't fierce! It's a very easygoing rabbit and makes a great pet. Lionhead rabbits are happy living outdoors in a hutch or inside a house.

Most Lionheads have shorter hair on their bodies. This means they don't need too much **grooming**.

# Smooth and soft

These cousins of mine are just asking to be stroked. Look at how soft and velvety their fur is!

Rex rabbits make friendly pets and are good at **adapting** to different situations.

## Rex rabbits

The Rex **breeds** are a group of rabbits who have a special velvety coat. These rabbits don't have the longer "**guard hairs**" that other rabbits have in their coats. This makes their fur very firm and smooth to stroke. Standard Rex rabbits are a medium size, while Mini Rexes are small. Rexes can be a variety of colours, including black, white, grey-blue, and patterned.

# Thrianta rabbits

Thrianta rabbits have beautiful, soft fur. Their coats are a rich, bright golden red colour and they have dark brown eyes. These medium-sized rabbits are stocky and solid, with small heads and furry ears. Thriantas love the outdoors and their friendly and easygoing nature makes them easy pets to keep.

The Thrianta rabbit's brightly-coloured fur makes it stand out from other pet rabbits.

# Flopsy bunnies

## English Lop rabbits

Have you ever seen a rabbit with ears this big? No wonder they can't stick up! English Lop rabbits' ear-span can be longer than 50 centimetres (20 inches), larger than any other **breed** of rabbit. English Lop rabbits are large and need a lot of looking after to keep those ears healthy. They like living indoors and can be calm and friendly pets, although they don't like being picked up very much.

Some of my relatives have floppy ears! They're called lop eared rabbits. Let's find out about some of them!

The English Lop rabbit was a popular pet in Victorian times.

# Cashmere lops

Cashmere lop rabbits are medium-sized and have very long, soft coats. They have large heads and fairly small lop ears. Cashmere lops are gentle and relaxed rabbits and are lovely to hold and stroke, but their long coats make them difficult pets to keep. **Bedding** can get tangled up in their fur and their hair needs to be **groomed** every day.

Cashmere lop rabbits can have fur in many different colours.

# Giant cousins

Some of my relations are massive! Here are a couple of the biggest.

Flemish Giant rabbits reach their full size just before they are a year old.

## Flemish Giant rabbits

Flemish Giant rabbits are a very old **breed** that started out in Belgium. This huge rabbit can weigh more than 5 kilograms (11 pounds). It has dark grey fur, a long body, and strong back legs. Flemish Giants tend to be **docile** and enjoy being **handled** gently. Because it's so big, the Flemish Giant needs plenty of food and exercise.

# Continental Giant rabbits

If you thought the Flemish Giant was big then check out this monster! The Continental Giant can weigh 9 kilograms (20 pounds) and has a large and powerful body and head. Even its ears are huge! These gentle giants are very friendly and affectionate pets but you need to have plenty of room to keep them! They need an extra-large hutch and **run**, and like the Flemish Giant, they need lots to eat.

## FAMILY SECRET

The females in some breeds of giant rabbits sometimes have a dewlap. This is a large fold of skin under their chin. It helps to make them look even bigger!

The Continental Giant is the biggest rabbit breed of all.

# little friends

Netherland Dwarf rabbits are not much bigger than a kitten, even when fully grown!

Now we go from big to small. These little cousins of mine are tiny! Let's take a closer look.

## Netherland Dwarf rabbits

The Netherland Dwarf is the smallest **breed** of rabbit. Netherland Dwarf rabbits have large heads compared to their little bodies. Their ears are very small and stick up straight. This little rabbit is a very popular pet. It's easy to look after and doesn't need too much space to run around, although it is very active.

# Miniature Lop rabbits

The Miniature Lop is a fairly new breed of rabbit. This little bunny can weigh up to 1.6 kilograms (3½ pounds) and has a very sweet nature. Miniature Lops are solid, with a large head and wide, rounded ears. They are curious and enjoy playing and cuddling up with humans. They make great pets and can even be trained to use a **litter tray**.

Miniature Lop rabbits are most active and playful in the morning and evening.

# Part of the family?

Hmmmm. These animals don't sound like rabbits. But despite their confusing names, they really are part of my family.

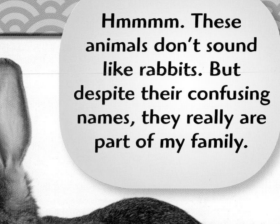

Belgian Hares make friendly pets but they can be hard to catch and pick up!

## Belgian Hares

It's called a hare but it's a rabbit! The Belgian Hare gets its name because it looks a bit like a wild hare, with its arched back and long ears and legs. It has beautiful short fur in a deep red or brown colour and large eyes. Belgian Hares are clever and energetic so they need plenty of space to run around.

# Chinchilla rabbits

Is it a chinchilla or a rabbit? Well, it's a rabbit, but it gets its name because its fur is so similar to the chinchilla. Chinchilla rabbits are large, with heavy coats in layers of colour that look stripy when stroked. Their fur is very soft and quite long. They are active and easygoing and happy living outdoors.

## FAMILY SECRET

Chinchillas are mouse-like animals that live in the mountains of South America. They used to be hunted for their thick, velvety fur. Today they are often kept as pets.

Chinchilla rabbits make excellent pets.

# Our growing family

All members of my family have a lot in common when it comes to bringing up babies. Let's look at life for young rabbits.

Baby rabbits are called kittens. Female rabbits, or **does**, are usually pregnant for around 30 days before giving birth to a **litter**. There are usually between three and nine babies in a litter. The kittens cannot see or hear at first and they have no hair to keep them warm.

Baby rabbits huddle together to keep warm and need to drink their mother's milk for several weeks.

Baby rabbits are usually ready to leave their mother when they are around nine weeks old.

## Caring for young rabbits

After about five weeks, the kittens can be **weaned** off their mother's milk. They will have started to grow a coat of fur. They don't get their full adult coat until they are around six months old. It's a good idea to get a vet to **neuter** or **spay** a pet rabbit when it is young. This will stop the rabbit having babies.

## FAMILY SECRET

Pet rabbits can live for eight to twelve years. This is quite a long time, and anyone thinking about getting a pet rabbit should be ready to care for them for that long.

# Wild relations

Some of my relatives are seriously WILD! Here are just a few of them.

Tapeti rabbits have yellowy-brown fur.

## Cottontail rabbits

Cottontail rabbits live in North, Central, and South America. Most cottontails have small, white, fluffy tails, which give them their name. The Tapeti is a medium-sized cottontail rabbit that lives in South America. It is **nocturnal** and tends to live alone rather than in large groups. Tapeti usually live in forests and are also known as Brazilian Rabbits or Forest Rabbits.

Swamp rabbits eat reeds and other marsh plants. They can also swim!

## FAMILY SECRET

Many cottontails don't dig burrows like European rabbits. They will either shelter in shallow nests or find holes dug by other animals.

In the United States, cottontail rabbits include the Brush rabbit, the Swamp rabbit, the Mountain rabbit, and the Desert rabbit. Each of these rabbits has **adapted** to eat food and find shelter in its particular **habitat**. For example, Desert rabbits will eat cacti and don't need much drinking water. Cottontails run away from a **predator** in a zigzag line to confuse the animal running after them.

Here's one of my relatives who started out in Europe but has travelled all over the world. He isn't always welcome!

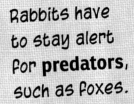

Rabbits have to stay alert for **predators**, such as foxes.

## European rabbits

The European rabbit started out in southwest Europe and northern Africa but it spread across Europe. European rabbits live in large groups and dig huge networks of burrows where they sleep and care for their young. These rabbits only tend to come out into the open in the early morning or evening. Grass is their main food.

## Unwelcome guests

In the past, European rabbits were taken to other parts of the world to be bred for meat. In countries such as Australia, they have caused problems because huge rabbit populations have destroyed many plants. This has led to **erosion**, which has damaged the land. A rabbit-proof fence was built in Australia to try to control the population, but it did not work.

Wild rabbits are not a welcome sight in some parts of the world.

# What type of rabbit are you?

If you were a rabbit, what type would you be? Try this quiz and find out!

**1. What is your hair like?**

a) Very long and needs lots of brushing

b) Short

c) Neither long nor short.

**2. Do you like getting lots of attention?**

a) Everyone notices you! You look so amazing people are always interested in you.

b) You don't mind – you're very easygoing

c) It depends what sort of mood you're in. People can be very annoying sometimes.

**3. How big are you?**

a) You're medium-sized but your hair makes you look bigger!

b) Huge!

c) Very small.

**4. Do you like being outside?**

a) You don't like to go outdoors much – you're usually indoors brushing your hair

b) You need lots of exercise so like to run around outside as much as possible

c) You don't mind being indoors or outdoors.

**5. How much do you eat?**

a) Not too much, not too little. You're just very careful not to get food in your hair.

b) Loads! Someone as big and active as you needs plenty of food.

c) Only as much as you need – you're only little.

## Answers

**Mostly a:** you are an Angora rabbit. You look amazing but your incredible hair needs lots of care, which doesn't leave you much time for other activities.

**Mostly b:** you are a Continental Giant rabbit. You're friendly and gentle and everyone comments on how big you are!

**Mostly c:** you are a Netherland Dwarf rabbit. People can be deceived by your cute appearance – you don't put up with anything you don't like!

# Glossary

**adapt** how animals change over time to suit their environment

**bedding** straw or other materials for an animal to sleep on

**blaze** coloured marking on the forehead of an animal

**breed** particular type of one kind of animal. For example, a Lionhead is a particular breed of rabbit. All the members of a breed are a similar size and shape, and they look alike.

**communicate** share information, ideas, or feelings with others

**docile** calm and gentle

**doe** female rabbit

**erosion** wearing away of land by sun, wind, water, or weather

**groom** clean an animal's fur

**guard hair** long, thick hairs at the top of an animal's coat

**habitat** particular environment where a plant or animal lives

**handle** pick up and hold

**hay** dried grass

**litter** number of babies born at one time

**litter tray** tray where animals can leave droppings and wee

**neuter** operate on a male animal to stop him having babies

**nocturnal** active during the night

**nutrients** parts of food that an animal's body needs to grow and stay healthy

**predator** animal that hunts and eats other animals for food

**run** closed-in area where animals can run and exercise

**spay** operate on a female animal to stop her having babies

**warren** network of rabbit burrows

**wean** introduce an animal to food instead of its mother's milk

# Find out more

## Books

*Rabbit* (Family Pet Guide), David Taylor (Collins, 2011)

*Rabbits* (A Pet's Life), Anita Ganeri (Heinemann Library, 2009)

*Rabbits* (Pets Plus), Sally Morgan (Franklin Watts, 2012)

*Rabbits* (See How They Grow), Kathryn Walker (Wayland, 2007)

## Websites

**animals.nationalgeographic.com/animals/mammals/cottontail-rabbit**
You can read more about Cottontail rabbits on this website.

**www.bbc.co.uk/nature/life/European_Rabbit**
Find out more about European rabbits on the BBC Nature website.

**www.rspca.org.uk/allaboutanimals/pets/rabbits**
The RSPCA website is full of interesting facts about rabbits and how to care for them. You can also find out about rabbit rescue centres and other organizations that care for unwanted rabbits and find them new homes.

# Index